MOSES

written by

Susan L. Lingo

Melissa C. Downey

illustrated by

Roy Green

STANDARD PUBLISHING
Cincinnati, Ohio

Scripture quotations designated by (ICB) are from the *International Children's Bible, New Century Version,* copyright © 1983, 1986, 1988 by Word Publishing, Dallas, Texas 75039. Used by permission.

Scripture quotations designated by (NIV) are from the *Holy Bible: New International Version,* © 1973, 1978, 1984 by the International Bible Society. Used by permission of Zondervan Bible Publishers and the International Bible Society.

Library of Congress Catalog Card Number 91-067045

ISBN 0-87403-914-2

Copyright © 1992 Susan L. Lingo, Melissa C. Downey
Published by The STANDARD PUBLISHING Company, Cincinnati, Ohio.
Division of STANDEX INTERNATIONAL Corporation. Printed in U.S.A.

Moses

"All Hebrew boy babies will be killed!" declared the cruel Pharaoh, king of Egypt.

Jochebed heard the news and knew she had to save her baby. She kept her precious son a secret for a while, but she soon realized that something else needed to be done. Jochebed carefully wove reeds together to make a basket. Then she put her baby boy inside the little basket boat. She and her daughter, Miriam, took the basket to the river and set it adrift. They hid in the reeds watching.

Just down the river was the pharaoh's daughter and her servants. When Pharaoh's daughter saw the basket, she was curious. She waited at the water's edge as her servants brought the basket to her. "A baby boy!" she exclaimed. Immediately she decided to keep him and raise him as her son. Miriam ran up to the princess and told her that she knew a woman who could help take care of the baby. The princess asked Jochebed to care for the baby. Jochebed knew in her heart

that it was God who had kept her son safe. This special baby was Moses.

After Moses became a man, he left Egypt and traveled to Midian where he became a shepherd. One day while Moses was out with his sheep, he decided to let the sheep graze near Mt. Horeb. While walking on the steep sides of the mountain, Moses looked up. "What is that burning over there?" Moses walked over for a closer look. A bush was on fire—but it did not burn up!

As Moses came near the bush, he heard a voice saying, "Moses! Moses! Take off your sandals, for you are on holy ground. I am the God of your father, the God of Abraham, Isaac, and Jacob."

God had heard the cries of His people, the Hebrews. The Hebrews were slaves to the people of Egypt, and the Egyptians were very mean to them. God was sending Moses to lead His people out of Egypt and into the land God first promised to Abraham.

Moses returned to Egypt and told the Pharaoh that God had commanded that all of the Hebrew slaves be set free. Pharaoh did not believe what Moses said. Pharaoh's heart was hard. God punished Pharaoh and the Egyptians with many bad things. He ruined all the water; He filled the land with frogs, gnats, and flies; He killed the cattle; and He caused the people to break out in a rash. Then He sent hail from the

© 1992 Susan L. Lingo, Melissa C. Downey
Permission is granted to reproduce this page for classroom use only—not for resale

sky to beat down the plants and sent locusts to eat what was left in the fields. He sent darkness to last for days. Each time something bad happened, Pharaoh refused to follow God's commands. Finally, all the firstborn of Egypt died, including Pharaoh's own son. The people of Egypt were so unhappy that Pharaoh at last let the Hebrew people go free.

The Hebrew people quickly packed and left Egypt. However, before they had gone very far, Pharaoh changed his mind again. He followed the Hebrews, wanting to bring them back to slavery. Pharaoh chased them to the shores of the sea; but God moved the water so His people could cross on dry ground. But when the Egyptians tried to cross, the water came crashing down.

With Moses as their leader, the Hebrews traveled through the desert. Every day God met their needs. God showed them the way to go with a pillar of clouds in the day time and a pillar of fire in the night time. God sent them manna and quail to eat. He even gave them water from a rock to drink. In all ways, God took care of His people.

As their leader, Moses was given laws for the people to follow. God gave Moses ten laws for them to learn and to always obey. These ten laws are the Ten Commandments.

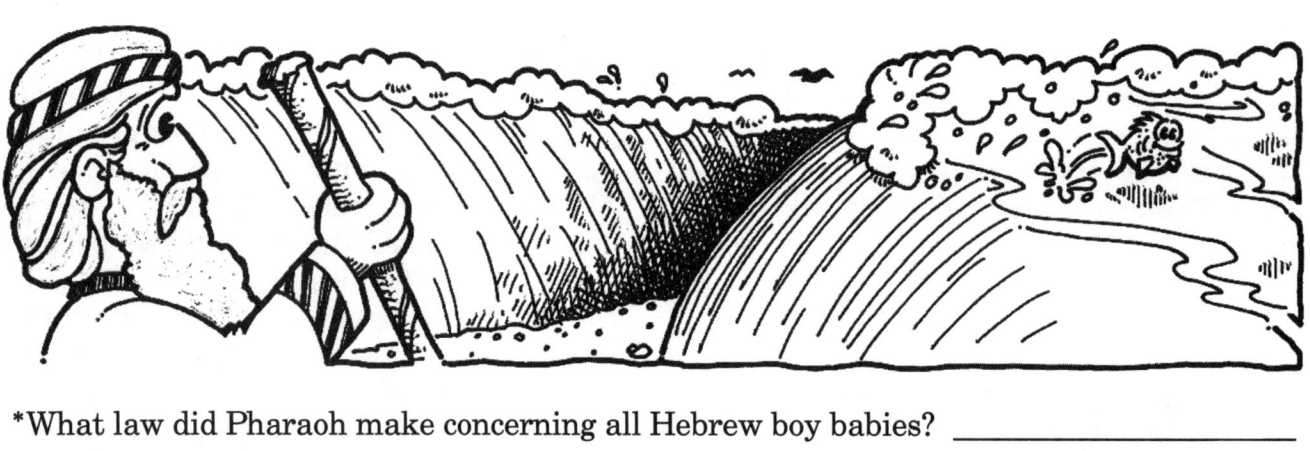

*What law did Pharaoh make concerning all Hebrew boy babies? _____
_____

*What did Moses see up on the mountain as he was tending his sheep? _____
_____

*What were some of the bad things that happened to the Egyptian people because Pharaoh would not let the Hebrews go? _____
_____

*Name ways that God took care of His people in the desert. _____
_____

*What were the ten laws that God gave His people called? _____

© 1992 Susan L. Lingo, Melissa C. Downey
Permission is granted to reproduce this page for classroom use only—not for resale

Moses

Once there was a wicked 👑 in Egypt called Pharaoh. The bad 👑 made the 👥 of Israel slaves and wanted every 👶 boy killed. 1 👩 saved her 👶. She put the 👶 in a 🧺 and set it by a 🌊. The 👑 daughter found the 👶 and named him Moses.

When 🧔 grew ⬆️UP, he ran from Egypt. 1 day as he was watching his 🐑, God spoke to him from a burning 🌿. God wanted 🧔 to help free the 👥 of Israel. 🧔 was very afraid, but he loved God with all his ❤️ and obeyed.

🧔 told the wicked 👑 that God wanted His 👥 set free. At 1st the bad 👑 said, "NO!" But God punished the 👑, and he let 🧔 take God's 👥 from Egypt. 🧔 and the 👥 followed God's signs to the promised land. In the ☀️ they followed a pillar of ☁️, and at 🌙 they followed a pillar of 🔥. God led His 👥 to safety, and He gave them rules to live by.

🧔 and the 👥 thanked God with all their ❤️❤️ for His wonderful love!

© 1992 Susan L. Lingo, Melissa C. Downey
Permission is granted to reproduce this page for classroom use only—not for resale

Moses, May I?

"Observe the commands of the Lord your God, walking in his ways and revering him" Deuteronomy 8:6 (NIV).

This game is based on the old favorite, "Mother, May I?" Give it a new twist, and you can pretend to be the freed people of Israel trusting Moses to lead your every step from Egypt to the promised land!

1. Choose a player to be Moses. He/she will call the steps. Moses must stand opposite the players (about 20 feet away). Moses is in the promised land.
2. Players line up side by side. The players are in Egypt.
3. Moses will call on one player at a time and tell him how many steps of faith he may take. (Steps are described below.) Example: Take 3 Noah steps.
4. Player must ask: Moses, may I? before he takes his steps. If he forgets to ask, he must go back to Egypt until his next turn.
5. First player to the promised land is the winner and will be Moses for the next game!

Steps of faith:

ABRAHAM STEP:
Close eyes (and trust!). Take 1 step back and 2 steps forward.

NOAH STEP:
Like the rabbits on the ark, Noah's step is 1 hop!

BABY ISAAC STEP:
Take 1 baby step while laughing.

GOLIATH STEP:
Take 1 giant step.

Did You Know?

Children of Moses' time played nine pins, a game much like our bowling. They had toys with moving parts, like chariots and wheeled carts, or puppets with arms and legs that moved. Children would go bird hunting with a throw stick (similar to a boomerang). Instead of a dog, they'd use a cat to fetch the birds!

When children were sick, they didn't take aspirin or other medicines that we might use. They might have to take a mixture of boiled beetle and animal fat.

© 1992 Susan L. Lingo, Melissa C. Downey
Permission is granted to reproduce this page for classroom use only—not for resale

"This was the time when Moses was born. He was a fine child. For three months Moses was cared for in his father's house. When they put Moses outside, the king's daughter took him. She raised him as if he were her own son. The Egyptians taught Moses all the things they knew. He was a powerful man in the things he said and did."

Acts 7:20-22 (ICB)

Picture Words
Using the examples in the boxes as a guide, draw a picture to illustrate each of the missing words below.

"This was the _____ when _____ was born. _____ was a fine _____. For three months _____ was cared for in his father's _____. When they put _____ outside, the _____ took him in. She raised him as her own son. The _____ taught _____ all the things they knew. He was a powerful man in the things he said and did.

All in Good Time
Place the following events in Moses' life in the correct order by writing a "1" by the first event, a "2" by the second event, and so on. Use the Scripture above as a guide.

_____ The Egyptians taught Moses all they knew.
_____ Moses was born.
_____ The king's daughter took him in.
_____ Moses was cared for in his father's house.
_____ Moses was a powerful man in all he said and did.

© 1992 Susan L. Lingo, Melissa C. Downey
Permission is granted to reproduce this page for classroom use only—not for resale

Most of the writing in Moses' day was done by scribes. Scribes were very important, educated people in the Egyptian world. They wrote down all important records.

When a scribe wrote, he used hieroglyphics, or picture writing. Each picture represented a sound. To make writing faster, they would sometimes leave out the vowels. For example, Peter would be PTR. Names of important people were placed in a special picture box called a cartouche. When the right pictures were added inside, the picture spelled the person's name. Make your own cartouche using the letters on the next page.

Moses studied reading, writing, and math just like you. His books were clay tablets written in hieroglyphics. Special books were written on papyrus paper and rolled on scrolls. How did the people in Moses' day get this paper to write on? They made it by hand using the following recipe—

Recipe for: paper

From: an Egyptian friend

Ingredients: papyrus reeds, flat stone, wet cloth, mallet, rounded stone

Cut papyrus reeds into very thin strips and lay them in rows on a flat stone. Then put another layer on top of the first row, this layer going across the first. Place a wet cloth on top and pound the two rows together with a mallet for an hour or two or until the strips are matted together to form one sheet. Next press the sheet under a heavy weight until flat. Dry in the sun. Polish with a rounded stone and trim for straight edges.
Yields: one sheet of writing paper.

© 1992 Susan L. Lingo, Melissa C. Downey
Permission is granted to reproduce this page for classroom use only—not for resale

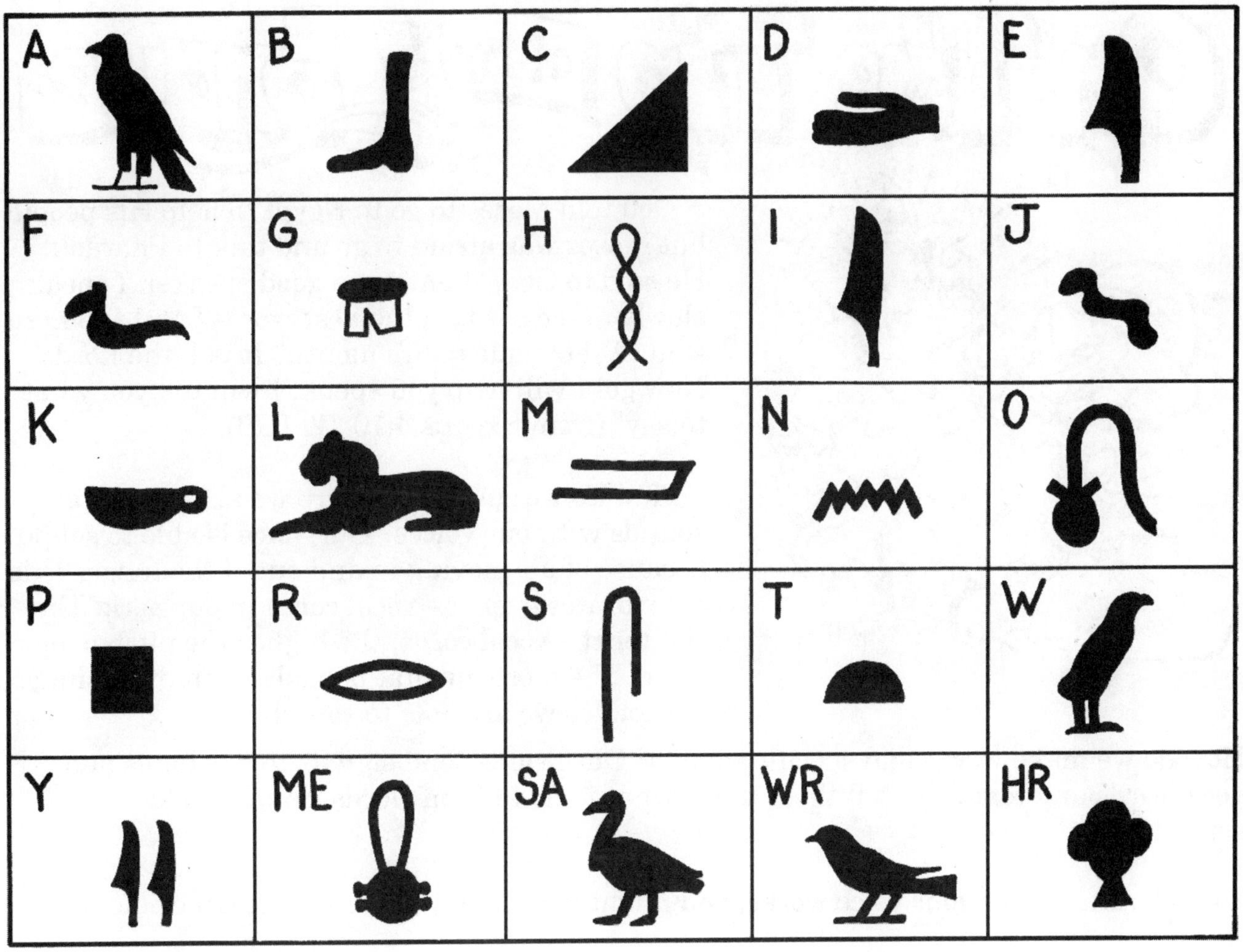

Using the hieroglyphic alphabet above,
translate the following Bible verse.

"__ ___ ___ ___ ____

___ _____."

Ecclesiastes 12:13 (ICB)

© 1992 Susan L. Lingo, Melissa C. Downey
Permission is granted to reproduce this page for classroom use only—not for resale

On The Tip of My Tongue

God told Moses to go to Egypt to help His people, but Moses was afraid to go and talk to Pharaoh. He said to God, "I am not a good speaker. I speak slowly and can't find the best words." But the Lord said, "Who made man's mouth? It is I, the Lord. Now go! I will help you speak. I will tell you what to say" (from Exodus 4:10-12, ICB).

How *do* we speak? How are we able to make sounds with our voices? Our voice is able to sound because of air moving in and out of the lungs. This air vibrates over the vocal cords in our neck. The tighter the vocal cords, the higher the pitch of our voice. The more air that is pushed out of our lungs, the louder we are able to sound.

How do we make words and specific sounds? Our brains send signals to our lungs and vocal cords and tongue to tell these parts what to do to form words, sounds, and sentences.

To understand how your voice works, you might want to try these simple experiments:

1. Place your fingers on the middle of your neck. Now hum. Can you feel the vibration in your neck when you hum? This is caused by the air vibrating your vocal cords.

2. Now hum a very low note, then a higher note. Did you feel your neck move? This was your vocal cords loosening and tightening to make different sounds.

Because Moses felt tongue-tied, Aaron, his brother, spoke for Moses before the people. Try twisting and tying *your* tongue tightly with these tough tongue twisters!

- God's great grace gave good gifts!
- Pharaoh finally felt fear!
- Moses munched much manna in the morning.
- Live and love the Lord's laws.
- The Red Sea saw six slaves slip and slide!
- God made many mighty miracles!

"My tongue will speak of your righteousness and of your praises all day long."
Psalm 35:28 (NIV)

© 1992 Susan L. Lingo, Melissa C. Downey
Permission is granted to reproduce this page for classroom use only—not for resale

"CAN"fidence

"I can't do it!" cried John one day;
   he didn't think he could.
"I just can't DO it!" they heard him say;
   he didn't think he would!

John never thought he'd do it right
   and so he never tried.
He said, *"I CAN'T!"* both day and night;
   he pouted, fussed, and cried.

But there was One who knew John could,
   who said, **"Oh, yes you CAN!"**
He said, **"Have faith, dear John, you should lean on my helping hand!"**

And so John put his faith in Him
   and for the first time tried!
John's heart believed and leaned on Him;
   "I CAN! I CAN!" John cried.

I can do all things through Christ because he gives me strength.
Philippians 4:13, ICB

* Why didn't John even try to do anything?
* Who was the One who said to John, "Oh, yes you can!"?
* What can *you* do next time you want to say, "I can't!"?

The poem "CAN"fidence may be read in parts by teachers or older children for some extra fun! John's part is in italics, the narrator's part in standard print, and God's voice is in bold print. Make a simple puppet of John by following the directions below.

1. Color and cut out two faces for John—a sad face and a happy face.
2. Glue or staple faces on either side of a craft stick.
3. Show John's sad face during the reading of the poem, until you reach the last line—then show his happy face.

Let entire class read Philippians 4:13 together.

© 1992 Susan L. Lingo, Melissa C. Downey
Permission is granted to reproduce this page for classroom use only—not for resale

MIND MUSCLE: BATHMATH

You are a time traveler. You suddenly find yourself in ancient Egypt, a slave in Pharaoh's kitchen. The demanding cook yells for you to get the stuff he needs for the next meal and hands you a list. Using the chart below, can you figure out how much of each item you would need in our measurements?

1 omer of flour = _____

1 bath olive oil = _____

1 hin milk = _____

3 baths water = _____

1 cab meal = _____

Dry Measure

1 cab	2 pounds
1 omer	4 pounds
1 seah	14 pounds

Liquid Measure

1 bath	6 gallons
1 hin	4 quarts (1 gallon)
1 log	1/3 quart

Did You Know?

What do you think of when you hear the word "bath"? We usually think of bathing, using soap and water in the bathtub, in the bathroom, right? Well the Hebrews thought of a big jar of water—six gallons. Over the years (hundreds of years), the meaning of the word has changed from being a measure of water to washing one's self. So . . . how many baths does it take to take a bath?

© 1992 Susan L. Lingo, Melissa C. Downey
Permission is granted to reproduce this page for classroom use only—not for resale

Needed for each fan:

poster board
string
glue or stapler
varnish (optional)
markers
large tree leaves or leaves
  made of construction
  paper

1. Collect large leaves. Press them for three to four days under a flat, heavy object. (Or cut leaves from construction paper using real leaves as a pattern.)

2. Paint both sides of leaves with clear varnish (optional).

3. Cut two handles for each fan from poster board or heavy construction paper.

4. Glue or staple the leaves to one of the handles being careful to line up the stems of the leaves with the handles.

5. Wrap the handles with string.

6. Use markers to decorate the handles.

© 1992 Susan L. Lingo, Melissa C. Downey
Permission is granted to reproduce this page for classroom use only—not for resale

When Pharaoh refused to obey God's command to let the children of Israel leave Egypt, God sent ten plagues upon the Egyptian people. Complete the puzzle to discover what these ten plagues were.

All of the boxes connect with a box containing the same letter. After you finish the puzzle, check your work in Exodus 7—11.

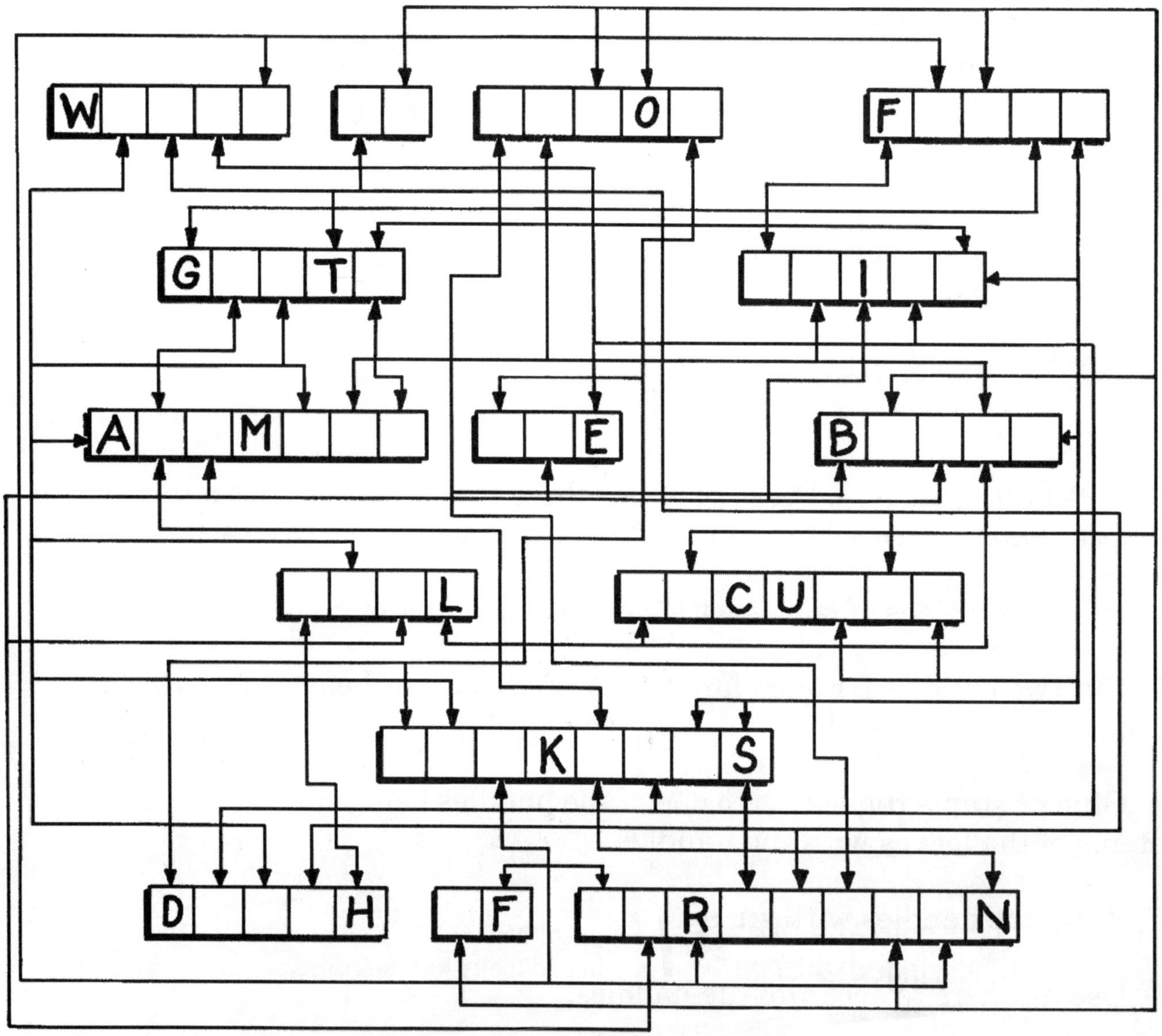

© 1992 Susan L. Lingo, Melissa C. Downey
Permission is granted to reproduce this page for classroom use only—not for resale

Riddle Me This...

Look at the riddles on the left. See if you can discover the answer before looking at the information on the right. Each answer is one of the plagues God sent to Egypt.

What am I?
I live in water and on land.
I keep my skin as wet as I can.
I lay my eggs in water to hatch.
I am really very hard to catch.

What am I?
I am the pollen-spreader and the ceiling-walker.
I am the germ-carrier and the winged-biter.
I am the picnic-spoiler.
What am I?

What am I?
I am a farmer's dread,
    The swarming crop-destroyer.
Using my legs like violins,
    I am a melody-maker.
I am an egg layer,
    A six-jointed jumper.
Against Pharaoh I was
    God's winged-avenger.

Frogs are amphibians—they live both in water and on land. Some frogs are very small when grown, and others, like the bullfrog, can be longer than 18 inches (6-inch body, 12-inch legs). Bullfrogs can live as long as ten years.

God has given frogs neat ways to protect themselves other than just jumping. Some frogs can change their skin color to match their surroundings. And some frogs have poison on their skin to keep enemies from eating them.

Frogs have long sticky tongues for catching their food. In a flash, a frog can stick out its tongue and catch an insect. One problem though—that doesn't work under water.

Those pesky little insects God sent to plague the Egyptians are a wonder! Did you know that flies can fly upside down? And they can fly at up to five miles an hour.

Why are flies so nasty? Flies have very sticky legs and feet which help them walk on the ceiling. But these same sticky feet spread germs. Everywhere flies walk or land germs and dirt stick to their legs and feet. And when the flies fly away, these germs go with them until they land again.

All through the Bible locusts are looked on as symbols of destruction and woe. They were also a source of food, however. In the New Testament we read about John the Baptist's meals of locusts and wild honey.

Locusts live in nearly all parts of the world where there are green plants—their source of food. Sometimes millions of locusts gather in "hordes" and begin to move across the countryside eating *all* green plants in their path! Not one leaf or blade of grass is left! The horde looks like a shimmery cloud as it drops to earth, blotting out the sun.

© 1992 Susan L. Lingo, Melissa C. Downey
Permission is granted to reproduce this page for classroom use only—not for resale

Hidden Locusts

Both Egyptians and God's chosen people were used to seeing locusts (although not in the numbers God sent to plague Egypt!). Artists usually painted things they saw in everyday life. In this Egyptian painting, how many locusts are you able to find?

© 1992 Susan L. Lingo, Melissa C. Downey
Permission is granted to reproduce this page for classroom use only—not for resale

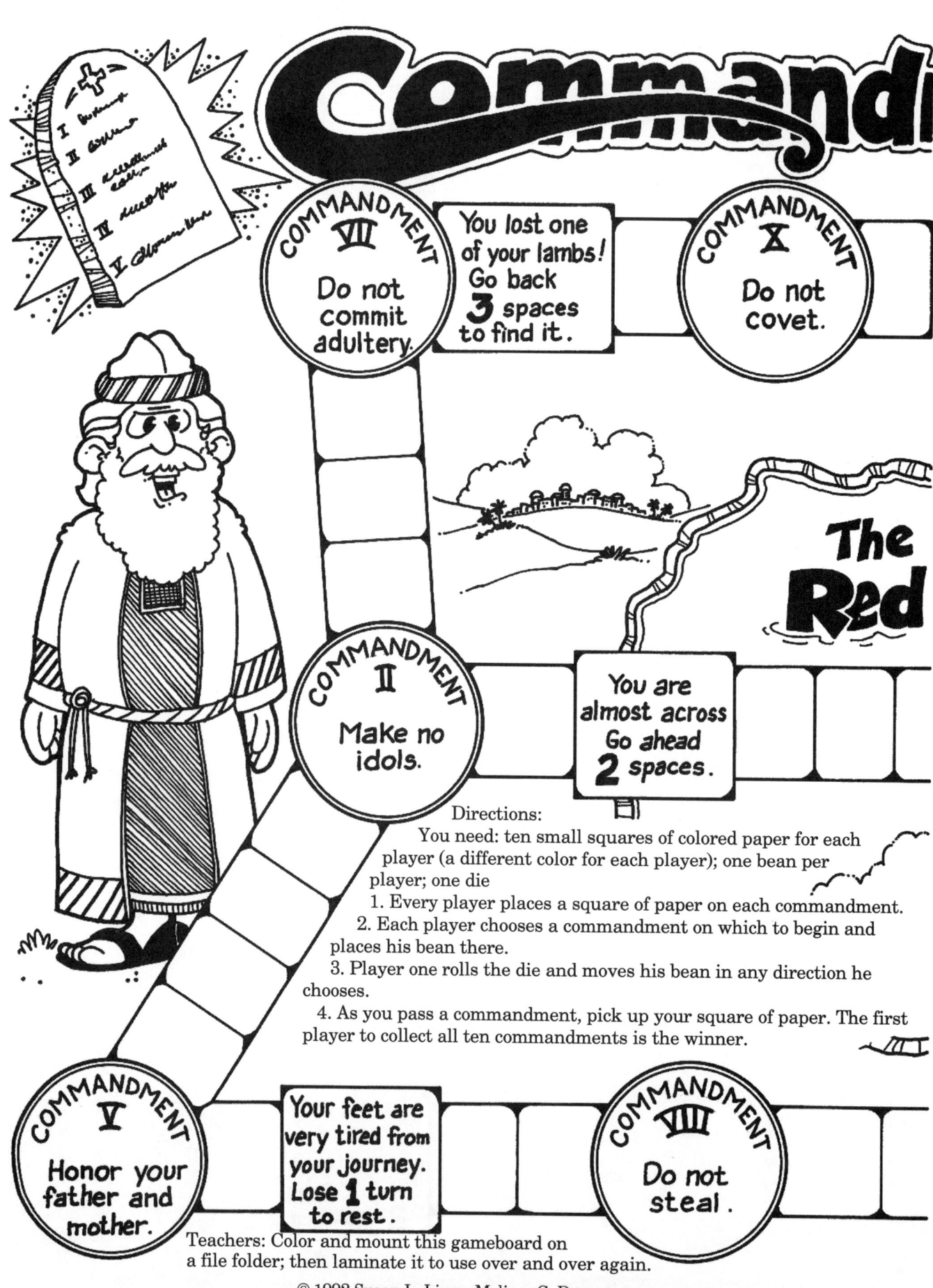

Wilderness Wanderings

You can complete the map! First, match the numbers on the map with the numbers in the boxes on this page. Next, write the name of the place in the blank next to the number. Now, map the wandering of the Hebrews by drawing a line connecting the numbers. To finish, color the map.

Map labels:
- The Great Sea
- Dead Sea
- 9 Mt. Nebo
- 1 Rameses
- 8 Kadesh-Barnea
- 2 The Crossing of Sea
- 3 Marah
- Wilderness of Sin
- 4
- 5 Rephidim
- 6 Mt. Sinai
- 7 Hazeroth
- Red Sea

1 ____
Moses leads the people out of Egypt.
Exodus 12:37

2 ____
God parts the waters of the sea.
Exodus 14:21-22

3 ____
Bitter water was made sweet here.
Exodus 15:23-25

4 Wilderness of ____
God fed the people manna and ____.
Exodus 16:13-18

5 ____
Water from a rock
Exodus 17:1-6

6 ____
10 Commandments given here.
Exodus 20

7 ____
More food given.
Numbers 11:31-33

8 ____
Spy mission
Numbers 13:23-25

9 ____
Moses saw the Promised land from here.
Deuteronomy 34:1-6

© 1992 Susan L. Lingo, Melissa C. Downey
Permission is granted to reproduce this page for classroom use only—not for resale

You are hungry and God has promised you food. God always keeps His promises, and, sure enough, you wake up one morning and find a sticky cotton-like "stuff" clinging to the bushes and ground and are told this is your bread from heaven! "What *is* it?" you ask, as you look around. It's manna! The Hebrew word for "what is it?" is manna.

See if you can make a picture of that first "manna morning" using the suggestions given below. Or perhaps you'd like to cook up your own version of manna by following the manna "recipe" at the bottom of the page.

You need:
soap flakes
water
bowl
electric mixer
blue construction paper
crayons

1. Whip soap flakes and water until they are stiff.
2. Draw the ground, bushes, and whatever you would like to see in your picture.

3. Use your fingers to dab soap flakes onto the bushes and ground.
4. Let your picture dry, and then you can actually feel the "manna" of the morning!

MANNA

You need:
3 T honey
1/2 bag marshmallows
10 graham crackers

1. Melt marshmallows and honey together. Stir well!
2. Put graham crackers on a cookie sheet.
3. Dribble "manna" over graham crackers and chill in refrigerator 1/2 hour (or more).
4. Enjoy your "manna"! (Makes 10 servings.)
Remember! Manna was sticky, and so is this. Use a napkin!

© 1992 Susan L. Lingo, Melissa C. Downey
Permission is granted to reproduce this page for classroom use only—not for resale

AMAZE-ing Grace

God showed His chosen people amazing grace when He used Moses to lead them out of Egypt and into the promised land!

See if you can find the path from Egypt to the promised land in the maze below.

© 1992 Susan L. Lingo, Melissa C. Downey
Permission is granted to reproduce this page for classroom use only—not for resale

COMMANDMENT CROSSWORD

Use Deuteronomy 5:5-22 (NIV) to solve the puzzle.

ACROSS

1. You shall have no other ____(s) before me (5:7).

3. You ____ not murder (5:17).

4. God brought His people out of ____ (5:6).

6. Six days you shall ____ (5:13).

7. false testimony; fib (5:20)

8. liquid used to annoint

9. the Red ____

10. Observe the Sabbath day by keeping it holy ____ the Lord your God has commanded you (5:12).

13. ____ your father and mother (5:16).

14. nickname for James

15. belongs to me

16. You shall not misuse ____ name of the Lord (5:11).

17. ____ am the Lord your God (5:6).

18. You shall have ____ ____ gods before me (5:7).

DOWN

1. God told Moses to ____ up the mountain.

2. A book of the Bible that has the Ten Commandments.

3. another word for rob

5. ____ received the Ten Commandments from God.

6. . . . so that you may ____ long (5:16)

7. I am the ____ your God (5:6).

9. Observe the ____ day (5:12).

11. ____ me and keep my commandments (5:10).

12. You shall not ____ your neighbor's wife (5:21).

13. opposite of her

© 1992 Susan L. Lingo, Melissa C. Downey
Permission is granted to reproduce this page for classroom use only—not for resale

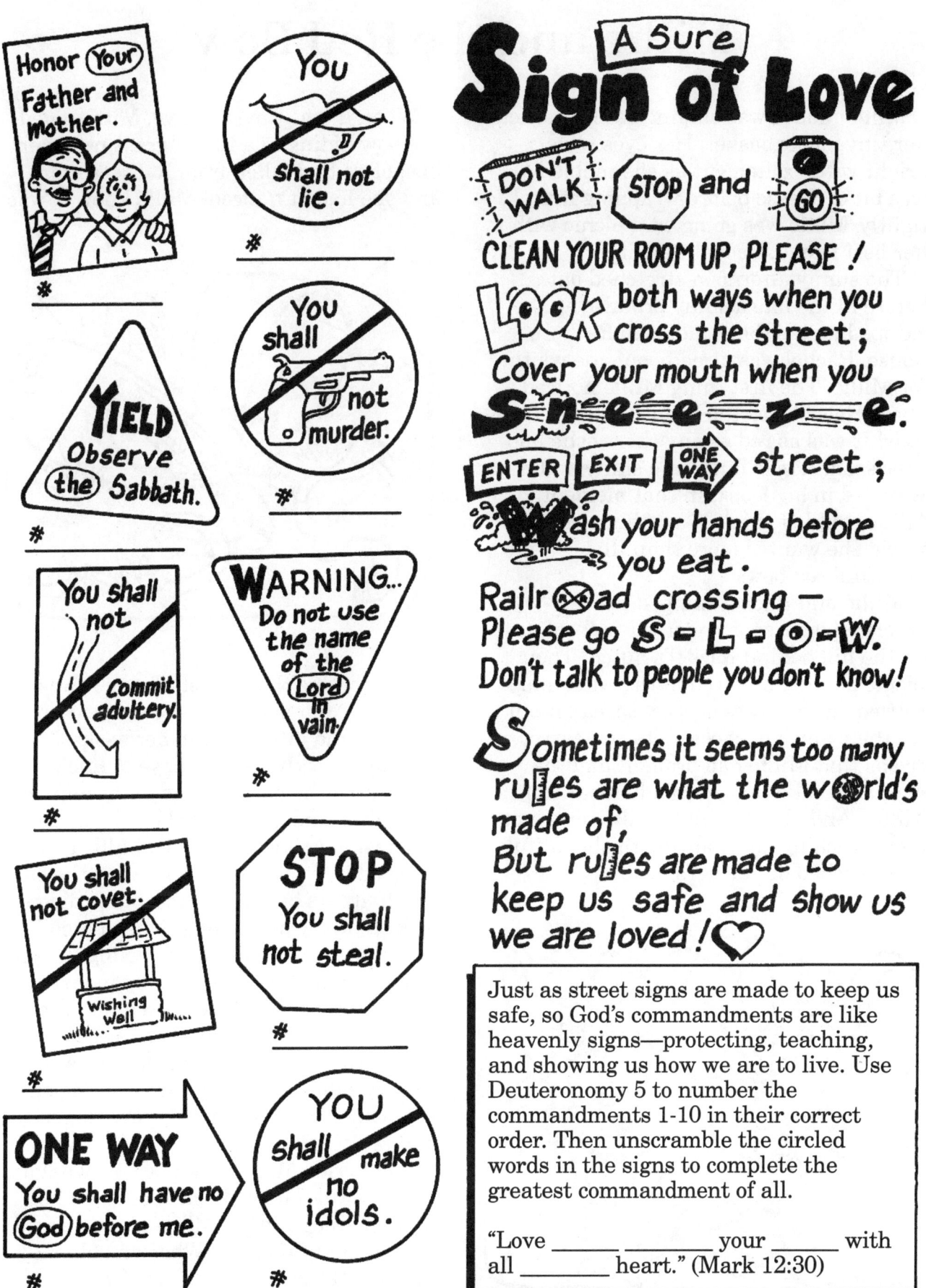

Millie and the Red Bow

Millie Mouse was singing as she packed her tiny picnic basket. Her eyes were bright with excitement as she nibbled a wee bit of cheese before wrapping it up tightly. Millie was going on a picnic with her best friend, Rachel Rabbit.

The sunny afternoon stretched out before Millie like a shiny promise as she skipped across the meadow to Rachel's house. Rachel was already outside waiting for Millie. The first thing Millie noticed about Rachel was the beautiful bow in her hair! It was as red as any cherry she had ever seen. It was fluffy and shiny and it was tied in big loops! In that moment, Millie couldn't think of anything in the world she wanted more than that beautiful red bow!

Millie and Rachel skipped to their favorite picnic spot under the tall oak tree on the hill behind Rachel's hutch. Their picnic blanket billowed in the wind and settled on the grass as they spread it out for their lunch of cheese bits and carrot crisps that Millie had brought and the chocolate cake that Rachel had baked for Millie. And all the while, Millie could not stop watching and wanting the beautiful bow perched on Rachel's head!

When it was time to leave, Millie spied the bow hiding in a tuft of grass near her basket. It had fallen from Rachel's hair and she hadn't noticed! Millie knew it was

wrong to take the bow; she *knew* it was wrong . . . but suddenly, she scooped up the bow and dropped it in her basket!

Millie quickly said goodbye to Rachel and ran for home. She flew in through her front door and gasped for breath as she set the basket on her tiny table. Millie gently reached into the basket and lifted the bow to admire its beauty. Funny, but it did not look as pretty as she had remembered. And what was this strange feeling tugging at her tummy? She reached up to fasten the bow in her hair and looked into the mirror expecting to see the most beautiful bow in the world. Instead, she saw a bow that was dull and sadly sagging. The once-beautiful bow wasn't pretty any longer, and Millie felt sick inside.

"Oh!" cried Millie, "I know now what a wrong thing I have done!" She hung her head. Through tears, Millie quietly asked, "What shall I do now? Who can help me? Perhaps if I pray to the Lord, He will

© 1992 Susan L. Lingo, Melissa C. Downey
Permission is granted to reproduce this page for classroom use only—not for resale

speak to my heart and tell me what to do." Millie, a small gray ball of unhappiness, bowed her head and prayed.

Almost at once, her heart began to speak to her! In that instant, Millie knew why God tells us not to steal! Because of His great love for us, He knows that stealing hurts not only others but ourselves as well. Millie knew what she must do and scampered, with the bow, to Rachel's house.

Rachel came to the door in tears. "Millie, I cannot find my favorite bow anywhere. I must have lost it on our picnic!" Millie gulped. God was right; stealing *does* hurt. Both she and Rachel were hurting!

Millie took a deep breath and handed Rachel the bow. "R-r-rachel, I took your bow. It was so pretty that I wanted it for myself. I was wrong, and I am so sorry! Will you forgive me? Are we still best friends?"

Rachel's eyes filled with sunshine and she forgave Millie. They were still best of friends! Millie's heart swelled with love for her very best friend who loved her enough to speak to her heart . . . God!

* How did Millie feel when she did something she knew was wrong? _____

_____

* How did praying help Millie? When do you go to God in prayer? _____

_____

* What did Millie learn about stealing and about God's great love for her? _____

_____

* Have you ever forgiven anybody or have you ever been forgiven? Tell about how you felt. _____

"You shall not steal" Deuteronomy 5:19 (NIV).

© 1992 Susan L. Lingo, Melissa C. Downey
Permission is granted to reproduce this page for classroom use only—not for resale

God's Word

Have you ever felt alone or afraid and wanted someone you love close to you? God has promised to always be with us—we are *never* alone!

Memorize the following verse, and then make the Heart of God necklace described below. Wear it close to your heart to remember that God is forever near.

"God said, 'I will be with you'" Exodus 3:12 (ICB)

You need:
* pre-cut wooden heart (from craft store) or use the pattern below to cut a heart from a plastic milk jug
* red markers or paint
* ribbons, buttons, glitter, etc. for decoration
* yarn or fishing line
* paper punch

Use the markers or paint and other items to decorate your heart. Glue a piece of paper with the Scripture from Exodus 3:12 printed on it to the center of the heart. Punch a hole in the top center of the heart. Cut a piece of yarn or fishing line long enough to go over your head and hang loosely around your neck. Thread the yarn through the hole and tie it. Allow your necklace to dry before wearing it.

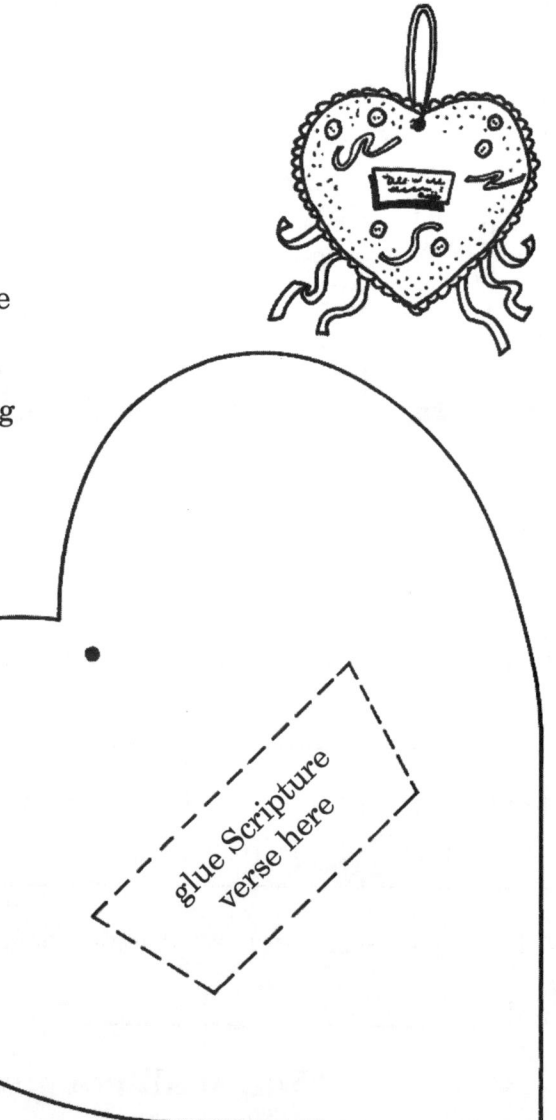

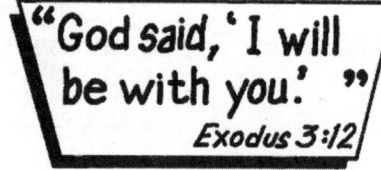

© 1992 Susan L. Lingo, Melissa C. Downey
Permission is granted to reproduce this page for classroom use only—not for resale

Commandment MATCH UP

1. Cut out cards and mix them up.
2. Place cards face down in four rows.
3. The first player turns over two cards. If they match (commandment with its correct number), he keeps the pair. If they do not match, he turns them back over and the next player takes his turn.
4. The player with the most matched sets is the winner!

(Teacher: You may wish to photocopy this page before cutting it apart so you will have a ready list of the commandments and their chronological number.)

Commandment I	Commandment III	Commandment V	Commandment VII	Commandment IX
You shall have no other gods before me.	You shall not misuse the name of the Lord.	Honor your father and mother.	You shall not commit adultery.	You shall not give false testimony.
Commandment II	Commandment IV	Commandment VI	Commandment VIII	Commandment X
You shall not make for yourself an idol.	Observe the Sabbath day by keeping it holy.	You shall not murder.	You shall not steal.	You shall not covet.

© 1992 Susan L. Lingo, Melissa C. Downey

Permission is granted to reproduce this page for classroom use only—not for resale

Seek and You Shall Find

The words below are all a part of the story of Moses. See if you can find them in the box at the bottom of this page!

Moses	Mt. Horeb	leader
Egypt	Miriam	staff
locust	chosen	Pharaoh
trust	commandments	promised land
Aaron	Red Sea	burning bush

```
S P L R O T N H C
E R C E A R M P O
P O H M R U T H M
B M O M R S H A M
U I S I N T O R A
R S E R A A R A N
N E N I A F E O D
I D A A R F B H M
N L L M O S E S E
G A O E N A T O N
B N A C A R I M T
U D O E U D D P S
S E R E D S E A O
H E G Y P T T R M
S G V L R T W S L
```

© 1992 Susan L. Lingo, Melissa C. Downey
Permission is granted to reproduce this page for classroom use only—not for resale

**Open any window; open any door.
God has given us glorious gifts
to seek, to find, to explore!**

God's gift to Moses was the confidence to lead His people. Draw a picture of a gift God has given you.

© 1992 Susan L. Lingo, Melissa C. Downey
Permission is granted to reproduce this page for classroom use only—not for resale